# KEYS TO THE ONLINE DATING WORLD

## Easy steps you need to know before going into the dating world.

ISBN:9798847888288

# Table of Contents

# INTRODUCTION TO ONLINE DATING

There are a ton of things that an individual needs to be familiar with online dating before one gets into its complexities. Online dating might appear to be the least difficult thing on the planet however it isn't. It ought to be seen in all sincerity or things could go haywire. Each game has its standards and except if you know every one of the principles you can't turn into a decent player and in the long run a victor, just like my name. Smiles. Now let's get down to business.

## TASTE

There are such countless sorts of individuals around. Simply check them out. What number of individuals you know appear to be identical?

Sizes, shapes and features, they are so unique.

What's more, that is just about the outside appearances. With regards to character, it turns into an altogether different story at large. Go on an outing through a world of fond memories, return to your study halls and investigate.

A classroom is one place where we get to connect with a variety of individuals on an exceptionally close premise. We get share a building with different individuals and we get to know them on a balanced premise. So what number of your classmates did you truly like?

I don't mean like them as classmates but as individuals. Was it simple to coexist with every one of them? To that end we frequently end up with dearest companions in study halls.

We don't and don't need to like everyone. The preferences and interests of one individual could coordinate with our own while the preferences and interests of someone else might be at finished blockheads with our own.

So with regards to dating, it is a lot of a similar story. In any case, here there are a few surprises. Dissimilar to in a classroom contact, a great many people go on dates with a more noteworthy reason, and that is to find life mate. There are 101 things that ought to match before two individuals choose who to spend the rest of their life Is together.

Many individuals are of the assessment that they needn't bother with any assistance with dating. They might be correct on the grounds that no body understands an individual's preferences and likes better compared to the individual oneself.

Perhaps the majority of us needn't bother with any assistance in settling on the ideal decision however isn't it great to get a couple of pointers on the dating system thusly, especially on Online dating? It is with this objective that this matter was arranged so the large numbers of people who are currently profiting of Internet dating might receive the best in return.

I that the vast majority of my readers are extremely bustling individuals who don't have much time to spend perusing a guidance manual.

So I have thought of something that requires only a glance to get the general idea. At the most you could require few minutes to run your eyes along the whole length of this book. It's just basic. And yet, don't allow the effortlessness to deceive you. For sure an exceptionally far reaching work means to leave no stones unturned.

You can either involve this book as a common principle to smooth out your match-hunting adventure, or you can continue to return to it to ensure each step before you really put your foot forward. I can guarantee you that assuming you utilize this book to direct you, there is no reason to be afraid by any means… you actually won't stagger.

# Why is Online Dating Different?

We people have been in this world for such a long time. Also, starting from the starting individuals have been picking accomplices. Societies across the world are altogether different and we can run over such countless various manners by which individuals pick their life mates.

Be that as it may, the idea of finding a soul mate with the assistance of the Internet is a genuinely good idea when contrasted and the history of humans. Obviously the Internet and PCs have impacted man's life such a lot of that it is nothing unexpected that in the questions of finding a reasonable accomplice as well, the Internet has made its presence felt.

Online dating is, to put is essentially or straight, finding a cooperate with the assistance of a machine in particular the PC through the Internet. That itself makes the thought and the cycle an extremely clever one to be sure, Hundreds of cheerful individuals across the globe have been fruitful in tracking down reasonable accomplices by the method for online dating.

Be that as it may, frankly, a ton of not-really fortunate people have been goofed and abandoned by a similar cycle. So to ensure that you find a spot in the principal list let us delve into the subtleties of Online dating.

## INTERNET TRICKS

All that applies to the Internet, applies to Online dating too. The Internet as we probably are aware considers limitless potential outcomes in correspondence, and this component has ended up being simultaneously the greatest shelter, as well as plague for Online dating.

Individuals can begin without any preparation and get to have a deep understanding of one another before the genuine gathering happens. Tastes and inclinations, different preferences, interests and fixations can be examined on a balanced premise so that while the gathering really happens these two individuals are not at all aliens to one another. Great, right?
And yet this opportunities for limitless correspondence leaves a great deal of room for cleverness too. Mankind is invested with an exceptional capacity to utilize, abuse and misuse exactly the same thing. What's more, normally, Online dating also has been and is as yet being utilized for wretched purposes.

The individual who is abusing this office may either be a reasonable joker or might be somebody with additional shrewd goals who is on a mission to get a few casualties. It is a result of this reason that a tad of schoolwork is great before you really hit the road.
However, you don't need to stress, the home work has proactively been meticulously finished for yourself and everything you need to do is run your eyes along the accompanying lines and you will be good to go to strike gold.

# WHAT MADE ONLINE DATING TREND

The explanation is basic. It is a lot of the very reason that the actual Internet turned out to be so well known. The Internet opens up an entirely different universe of correspondence and contact. What's more, the explanations behind this are given beneath.

- **Speed**

  With just a tap , you can send a message to another person thousands of miles away. You can be in your room and be having a video call on the go with leaving your room, unlike the old days where you will have to wait for days, weeks or even months just to send or receive a letter.

- **Privacy**

  You can be online chatting with someone without the person nearby knowing what's going on. You have total and absolute privacy. You can put a password on your phone thereby preventing anyone from reading your messages.

- **Chat History**

  You have no fear of loosing your messages, you can save them on your system or device memory, or better still you can save it on the cloud and have access to it whenever you want.

- **Options and Opportunities**

The Internet accommodates different choices like voice notes or face time.

You can see each other, converse with one another, and stand by listening to the person's voice, could you at any point consider a better start?

## KNOW WHY YOUR ARE ONLINE

We as a whole realize that man is a social being. Anyway man is likewise a desolate being. (Furthermore, when we say man, we mean ladies as well). Man yearns for company.

Spending quality time with friends and family, however from that unique individual with whom the person can share those romantic things, happy moments and torments, somebody with whom the person can fabricate an entirely different life, somebody with whom the individual can raise their very own family.

Presently this is a major need of man: to find a day to day existence mate. Furthermore, the most famous technique utilized for this is dating. At the point when we discuss dating in the extremely best feeling of the word, if it's not too much trouble, comprehend that dating isn't to be seen as a forerunner for having sex. It is significantly more than that. It is the most important move towards picking a soul mate and online dating has made the entire cycle much easier at this point.

# RELATIONSHIP VS MARRIAGE

Now what you do and what you want is entirely your business. I don't want to sound nosey but I would like to draw a fine line between the kind of dating that is involved in these two quests.

Of course we are all grown up and so let us act like grown ups. Obviously in a casual relationship we are looking for fun. And mind you, fun can have a lot of connotations. So here the object of one's desire will obviously be a person who is not inclined towards a serious relationship.

If both parties are of the same view then it is well and good because they understand each other perfectly and do not expect much from such a relationship. This leaves no room for heartbreak.

It is when one party is in for something more serious and the other party is into sheer frivolousness that the problems start. So you should be absolutely clear about what you are looking for from the start, and you should make your intentions very clear to the other person.
At the same time you should have no doubts about the intentions of the other person as well. Remember, even if it is a casual relationship, there should be mutual understanding at least about the nature of the relationship.

Of course, there is yet another possibility where a casual relationship can blossom into something more serious. But, again in such cases it is your instincts that can help you identify what is good and what is bad.

No matter how strong a person is, anyone can be taken for a ride or be taken for granted. Being jilted is never a nice experience. So those of you who are going in for a casual relationship, for heavens sake, be on your guard! Marriage is altogether a different story but we will deal with that later.


## DESIRE TO DATE

Can we just look at things objectively, obviously sex is significant, yet sex is by a wide margin NOT the main justification for dating.

Significant! Perhaps during the time of negligent youth, when new chemicals are being siphoned in and out, sex is on each one's brain. In any case, as one develops (mind you that doesn't mean becoming old and dim) sex takes the rearward sitting arrangement and common help, different preferences, collaboration, mindful and sharing come to the front. We fire pondering structure up our very own universe and we really want somebody to impart it to, and not only somebody to lay down with.

Sex is a key need of each and every person. We as a whole have it in us to give and get actual joy. In any case, when you sit and consider it briefly, you can see that this desire is really the aftereffect of another desire.

There is a more essential desire in each person to raise and create posterity, and this urge leads to such a strong sexual longing. However, whatever be the inclination, the most honorable means to fulfill it is dating.

No one, not one of us, is whole without a partner; and it is to fulfill this need that individuals date. Along these lines, the remainder of this manual will be devoted not to finding the right sex partner, but rather to finding the right soul mate.

## ONLINE DATING IS GOING NO WHERE

How about we acknowledge the way that dating can't actually improve. Online dating is THE genuine article. How about we contrast it with the old days from night balls or parties. Knowing fully well that you are in this large gathering where there are a great deal of people paying special attention to reasonable partners.

Assume you meet a couple of individuals with whom you appear to strike a prompt compatibility. You are then ready to take this individual out onto a gallery with no one to watch out for you.

You get to converse with this individual for a really long time; simply talk and that's it. You get to examine different preferences lastly when the time has come to part you leave with a guarantee to meet on a following day at a similarly charming spot. These discussions happen for a really long time lastly you conclude that this to be sure is THE individual with whom you need to use whatever is left of your existence with.

Then obviously you begin meeting at different spots, you hold each other's hands and even kiss. You start to go out for lunch and dinner and get to know each other. At the point when the time is right and your choice is made, it then, at that point, becomes time for you to say, "I do."

Hmm! It seems like a fantasy, isn't that so?

Well it shouldn't for even a moment need to be. It very well may be your own romantic tale in light of the fact that the idea of online dating exactly has been depicted previously. In the event that you check the right boxes, everything could turn out great for yourself.

The best thing about online dating is that it manages the cost of a great deal of protection. You can talk for quite a long time, video gathering, or do anything it is you want to manage without stimulating the interest of others or drawing in some unacceptable sort of consideration. All you want is a PC and Internet access everything becomes as cautious as anyone might think possible. However, alongside that, may I add that we really want a tad of sound judgment too or, more than likely we could end up inside the grasp of numerous shocking beasts prowling out there.

One more beneficial thing about online dating is that saves money, without you needing to empty your account each time you took somebody out. It is a direct result of these reasons and a lot more private reasons that a huge number of individuals view online dating as an extraordinary comfort.

## HOW TO UTILIZE ONLINE DATING TO YOUR ADVANTAGE

Many individuals who choose to check online dating out frequently end up with nothing to show for it

The explanation we chose to assemble such a manual is that online dating isn't quite so basic as it looks. You really need to know how to go about it to best out of it. The vast majority could do without to take risks and with regards to finding a day to day existence partner individuals would rather not take risks by any means.
Be that as it may, you can unwind for through this manual we will manage all the do's and the don'ts thus the entire interaction will be very simple and pleasant to you. This manual will give you bit by bit directions on the most proficient method to being online dating.

We feel a little wary about the critical thinking skills of our readers thus we don't propose to offer a ton of guidance on the issue. Our motivation is essentially to give few rules which we trust our readers will find important as they continue in the endeavor to track down the ideal partner.

# STEP 1: GETTING STARTED

It is best to thread carefully in a new environment. You want to be ready before you really go out there and begin to use your games. Make certain about yourself and make certain about what you need. Since everybody can compose anything they desire in a discussion channel doesn't imply that we need to do likewise.

The Internet is open to everyone. Yet, this equivalent quality draws in a wide range of individuals into it.

There are a ton of decent individuals utilizing the Internet, yet everything relies upon what you do. Do onto others how you believe they should treat you is also applies here. There are no guidelines for the game. All are players out there. Yet, on the grounds that others are hoodlums, it doesn't imply that you must be one as well. Your methodology is the main thing that can get you the sort of reaction that you need.

I don't feel that it is entirely reasonable to conclude that you can utilize the unexpected to get a date online. Simply by going into a discussion channel and saying "I'm free" you are just putting yourself available to be purchased, and will no doubt not obtain the outcomes you want.

One point that we all need to comprehend is that in a discussion board, all are equivalent. Try not to go by the misguided judgment that going into a discussion channel is like walking into a ball room wearing your best. Then, at that point, everybody goes to gaze at you and the most qualified individual (read that as the sexiest individual of the other gender) gets your attention and makes their direction towards you.

**WHERE TO BEGIN?**

The main tip we might want to give you isn't to go straight away into a singles' discussion channel and attempt to find someone who might intrigue you. We all know that the vast majority of such discussion boards are essentially overflowed with individuals who have just something single at the forefront of their thoughts - sex.
In this way, regardless of what you request, it generally winds up in that and the plan is crushed. You won't ever get the sort of individual who sort of matches your inclinations and tastes.

As such, it is the simplest thing to get somebody to lay down with you yet in the event that you are searching for something seriously persevering, similar to a partner forever, then you must be somewhat more quiet. The best of the lot isn't not difficult to track down. In any case, you in all actuality do track down it; being worth the effort is going.

So rather than going into a singles' discussion board, what you could do is, you could give the entire thing a shot from an alternate point. You could have a go at working in reverse.

**BEYOND WHAT THE EYES SEE**

Sit briefly and attempt and ponder the things that interest you and things that you would track down fascinating in an individual.

By 'things' here I am not alluding to physical qualities. I'm not alluding to something that could show you an individual's actual appearance. Again the qualification must be drawn between a committed relationship and a relaxed relationship. In an easygoing relationship, the significance is generally for the actual properties. We are more worried about what the individual resembles and what the individual has been invested with.

Then again, in the event that we have a committed relationship, the actual characteristics are not really significant. Similarity is likely the main variable here. Alongside that there are sure characteristics that clearly we will pay special attention to. We are discussing characteristics of the psyche. All things considered, external appeal is just superficial!

This thought could sound abnormal, yet it is valid. The thought is that it is feasible to develop to like the vibes of an individual. When you find the personality of the individual pleasant you will begin enjoying the individual in general. It is not difficult to imagine to experience passionate feelings for an individual in the event that the individual doesn't seem to be a celebrity. That is one of the stunts that nature plays.

There are many individuals who demand investigating the other individual's image before really focusing on a relationship. They could have their reasons obviously, yet I, as far as one might be concerned, feel that such a choice dependent to a great extent upon looks is more appropriate for a relaxed relationship. Sizzling off after some time is bound. All things considered, how long could you at any point continue to gaze at an individual? Also, what occurs in the event that the individual doesn't gaze back at you?

Or on the other hand far and away more terrible, what occurs assuming that you find the individual gazing at someone else? Looks might be significant, yet they unquestionably are not the main thing and ought to never be utilized as the game changer in the event that you are pondering a committed relationship.

## SHARED HOBBIES

A person isn't similar to a piece of glass however which you can look and see right through, An individual is more similar to a jewel, which when held against light mirrors and redirects light with the goal that a bunch of varieties are seen. We're perplexing.

We have a ton of interest and the interests of one individual need not coordinate with the interests of another. However, fortunately the interests are not quite so various as people. So we will undoubtedly find a many individuals who share our inclinations. What's more, in the event that we can find somebody like that, then our pursuit ought to end there. Anyway, what are your inclinations? That is something for you to find out.

Keep in mind, you could need to do some serious reasoning before you level down you inclinations. There may be a ton of things that you appreciate doing yet about which you have really thought about.

Your inclinations could be something like games or outside exercises. Or on the other hand you could imagine interests like social work or crosswords or strict interests. Keep the ball rolling; if it's not too much trouble, comprehend that the words I have recorded here are simple ideas.

Your preferences and interests could be totally different. So let them be. Also, whenever you have settled on what your inclinations are then a portion of the story is finished.

## WHAT YOU LIKE IN A PERSON

This is presumably the more significant piece of the story. Every single one of us needs to sit and contemplate what we would like in someone else. Having similar interests doesn't be guaranteed to imply that you can coexist with an individual.

For instance, assuming that you an individual who likes to gab, it doesn't imply that you could like someone else who likes to jabber too. In the event that two individuals attempt to continue to talk simultaneously, clearly, there can't be any exchange.

So additionally, assuming that you are the quiet saved type and the other individual also is the quiet held type, the there will barely be any exchange whatsoever! The word here is "viable." The interests of accomplices ought to complete one another and not conflict.

**KNOW THE RIGHT WORDS TO SEARCH**

So since you have concluded would could it be that intrigues you in an individual and what your inclinations and tastes are, attempt such watchword look through on a web crawler like Google.
The thought here isn't to promote yourself as an in individual hunt of a soul mate. Regardless of how well you put it, it looses that hint of nuance once you are in a singles' chat room. So don't do it that way. You recall how we talked about functioning in reverse; this is the way things are finished.

We will let you know how to project yourself best in a later part yet for the present let us discuss tracking down Mr. Right or Ms. Right. Something fascinating to be noted here is that it is easy to fall head over heels for an individual or to settle on a decision. The troublesome aspect is to pursue the best decision and to become hopelessly enamored with the ideal individual.

**DO'S AND DON'T'S**

The second thing that you could do is to write a rundown of characteristics that you really detest in an individual. Indeed I am not kidding! Disdains are similarly as significant, or considerably more significant than likes. We as a whole need to make splits the difference to a great extent, yet in the event that we start away by supporting things, which we truly hate, it will tell on the relationship at some point or the other.

I might want to give a fair warning here. A many individuals commit an error when they are pursuing. They set up their best way of behaving, which is excellent obviously, however they attempt to be very changing and it isn't awesome to accommodate which. A point that they will generally over look is that they won't be going on a setting up camp excursion with this individual that they are attempting to dazzle; they will be carrying on with their other lives with the individual.

So it is best not to be very "gracious so exceptionally accommodating and changing."

You can bear to adhere to things that you are extremely specific about. Furthermore, assuming that you have any contemplations that you will actually want to shape the individual out of their culpable propensities sometime in the future, fail to remember it.

The second you begin attempting to shape or wheedle the individual out of their propensities, anything they might be, the word becomes 'pestering' and if at all the individual drops the propensity, the person will cherish you less for it.

It truly doesn't work that way. So it's ideal to have an unmistakable thought regarding characteristics and propensities that you truly hate in an individual and avoid the 'lesser humans' who have those propensities.

When you have a genuinely clear thought regarding your preferences you are in a superior situation to settle on the ideal decision. Furthermore, taking into account the huge number of individuals out there, you don't need to stress or be over restless that you could very well not see as any one whatsoever. The person is out there, and assuming you are doing what you are doing well, in particular shooting for the right end goal you will succeed.

There are certain individuals who even accept that everything is appointed. It has been recorded who ought to wed who and in the end just that which ought to happen will occur. All things considered, I have hardly any familiarity with that, yet I in all actuality do realize that dating helps accelerate the cycle.

Something else that you could do is that you could just allow nature to follow through to its logical end. Goodness nature has its superb ways. There is a great deal of science engaged with the determination of accomplice so perhaps everything thing we could manage is loan nature some assistance.

**NO ONE SHOULD COME AHEAD OF YOUR FRIENDS**

Attempt to see this try not as a forthcoming spouse/wife chase but rather as a work to make a great deal of companions, and I mean old buddies. Companions that you can chuckle so anyone might hear with, companions who make you snicker. Not every person can make us chuckle, and when I say snicker, I am not alluding to some joke artist. We are discussing companions here.

It truly pays to have a great deal of companions. It makes ones life more extravagant. The best thing about companions is that you can act naturally with them. Also, they also can act naturally with you. What's more, that implies allowing everything to out. We should recollect that separated from being the obedient husband or wife, your life partner ought to be your dearest companion too.

That is one slip-up that most couples make. They will quite often view their companions and their life partners as discrete. While it is entirely alright to have your own companions, your dearest companion ought to constantly be your significant other or spouse.

It ought to be somebody you can impart your fantasies and fears to, somebody who gets it, somebody who can give your hand a delicate press when things turn out badly and somebody who can light up your most obscure day.

This is an extremely long ways from sex right? For that reason we referenced before that looks and sex ought to be the last rules in the determination of a soul mate. The engagement proposition should come as a characteristic grouping and it ought to in no way, shape or form be the primary thing that emerges when you heat up to an individual. You can't offer something like, "hello, you know what, I think we have similar preferences so we should get hitched."

You can express that obviously however it wouldn't be in excellent taste. So what do you do assuming you find that one of the companions that you made and the person who you were keeping your fingers crossed about is as of now hitched?

Do you have a vehicle? Then, at that point, the response is straightforward, just run over that individual's life partner and eliminate the undesirable component, correct? Wrong! It is simply not done. You can in any case be companions with that individual and change your consideration towards another course. Who knows, you could try and track down a superior individual. You should simply rearrange your cards and arrangement them out once more.

I want to believe that you have the hang of what we implied by working in reverse at this point? Great. There is one more catch engaged with this interaction. Quite possibly one of the companions that you made may have perused this book as well and perhaps the proposition might come from the opposite end.

In the event that it does, great; for it saves you the custom.

# MS. LEFT OR MR. RIGHT

However at that point, imagine a scenario where the individual who proposes to you wasn't actually what you had as a main priority. Indeed, the decision is yours obviously; you can live with or without it. In any case, there is a point worth thinking about here. On the off chance that we can find somebody that we cherish that is great, yet assuming we discover somebody who loves us, isn't unreasonably better?

However, I might likewise want to add a word here. Assume somebody really does come and propose to you however tragically, you are not at all intrigued? You reserve each privilege to turn the proposition down yet kindly do it smoothly. There is compelling reason need to hurt the other individual's self image. This individual is clearly a companion of yours, and without a doubt you care profoundly for them. Nonetheless, on the off chance that you realize that you can't wed this individual, a turned-down proposition is superior to a separation.

Attempt to make sense of your sentiments in the gentlest manner conceivable.

# STEP 2: WORKING ON YOUR APPEARANCE

No one is without flaws in this world yet that doesn't imply that we can't attempt to put our best self forward. There is literally nothing off-base in giving nature some assistance. Work on your picture, work on your profile, and work on your appearance.

Many individuals go by the way of thinking, "this is me, regardless of whether you like it's your concern. I won't change." Well, no one is requesting that you change, yet the thing would you say you are attempting to do? Frighten individuals away?

Indeed, the truth of the matter is, such proclamations are only your very own indication uncertainty. We as a whole have a specific level of uncertainty, certain individuals more than others. This instability makes us sound blunt and inhumane with regards to working on our appearances.

Come on, what are you scared of? I'll give you a tip. Anything that you fear, others fear exactly the same thing. In this world, the vast majority are neither as far as we're concerned nor against us. They are contemplating themselves.

Introducing oneself is a region that requires a great deal of work, however shockingly, this is the one region which individuals will generally disregard the most. A large portion of us have a laid back mentality with regards to laying out an image about ourselves. With regards to introducing yourself we truly have a work to do.

In the event that we knew you on a more private premise we would have wanted to assist you with chalking out a
profile of your self that sounds as noteworthy as could be expected, really. Obviously, knowing every one of our readers on a balanced basis is unimaginable.

Yet, you don't need to stress since we have done a ton of concentrate in such manner and when you follow our headings, you can for sure think of that dream profile.

**STUNNING PROFILE**

One can't take a lot of exertion in setting up a profile. It ought to be seen truly. Kindly don't treat the subject softly. Envision that you are planning for a task; could you invest a great deal of energy preparing your resume?

Indeed, the greater part of us take up positions for how long, four or five years? Furthermore, what about a relationship, certainly we don't leave on a relationship with the assumption that it would keep going for only several years.

We need to comprehend that a relationship is truly worth a lot in excess of a task, since it is likely the main choice in your life. So presently let us examine manners by which you can tidy up your profile.

You can obviously get an expert to finish the work for you since it saves you the work. You might need to dole out a modest quantity obviously, however everything will work out for the best. There are many individuals who have second thoughts about remembering an image for the profile. Indeed, I would rather not press the issue. It unquestionably improves to have an image in your profile, yet because of protection issues you can shun including an image.

Everything thing you could manage is once you are open to chatting with an individual and are persuaded that this individual has no naughty goals, you could send your image over as a connection or a document. However, this, as well, is best done a common trade premise. It would be unreasonable assuming that you understand what the other individual resembles however the other individual is kept in obscurity as well as the other way around.

**YOUR PICTURE**

Presently, coming to the image thusly, in the event that you are sending over an image of yourself, for God's sake, send over a nice picture. It ought to be a new one and kindly make no trade offs about the quality. Get an expert to finish the work for yourself and with the computerized methods of today, they can do an extremely noteworthy work.

Simultaneously take care of business on your appearance before the photo is taken. Stand before your mirror and evaluate different articulations till you get something that you believe is an ideal best for you. Furthermore, recall that it must be an image of you grinning. You shouldn't have the exemplary hang canine articulation, or the "margarine will-not-soften in-my-mouth articulation". Grin, it costs you nothing and it truly illuminates an individual's face.

Presently, the primary thing that you ought to do is take out a pencil and paper and record the crude insights concerning yourself. By crude subtleties we are alluding to things like you age, your level and your weight.

This is the skeleton of which we will chip away at. What's more, when we have added sufficient flesh to this spine, why even you will be dazzled by your profile! Yet, first let us avoid specific pit falls into which the vast majority fall.

## A FULLY PACKED PROFILE

The majority of us have been prepared to be extremely unobtrusive. With regards to praising our selves we have an extremely nauseous outlook on boasting. Right, no body is requesting that you really do any trumpet blowing yet realities must be expressed as realities.

In the event that you are a music sweetheart and have a decent voice as well, I can't understand the reason why you can't put it down like that itself. For what reason mightn't you at any point announce just without sounding exceptionally pleased that you have great voice? A pointer that you could endure as a top priority is add something like, "My companions believe that I sing rather well."

There now, you can't really regret something actually that straightforward.

So go on, on the off chance that you truly have an ability, you should as tell others about it, after each of the a gifted individual might a way want to be valued by an accomplice.

**BRAGGING**

Bragging, obviously, is a NO. So avoiding it is ideal.
This is particularly evident on account of actual characteristics. You may be one amazing looker, however let the other individual choose, recollect that the very thing that wine is for Peter can go of to be toxin for Paul.

You can offer suggested expressions like, "I'm surely not a terrible looker," or "assessment is separated, certain individuals feel that I am gorgeous while others feel that I am not." But maybe the most effective way of portraying yourself is add a bit of humor to it.

In the event that you are tubby you could express something like, "I'm round in the appropriate spots... I trust." If you are tall you could express something like, "some say I ought to play b-ball."

If you are on the short side you could express something like, "I could appear to ailing in size yet I guarantee you, it is by and large present."

You realize what is the most amazing aspect of such clever comments around oneself? Humor generally works. We all have been honored with a comical inclination somewhat in any event and in the event that an individual can offer entertaining remarks about oneself, that generally goes about as a turn on. Furthermore, you can believe me; humor sells like a billion bucks.

## PORTRAIT YOURSELF AS THE FUN TYPE

Attempt to make yourself sound as intriguing as could be expected. I would not joke about this. In the event that you are laying out a self representation you should utilize the right tones. Before we leave our homes what do we do? We as a whole spend something like five minutes before our mirrors trying to make our selves look as satisfactory and as noteworthy as could be expected.

Indeed, exactly the same thing applies to our profile. Eliminate all dreary insights concerning yourself that may be inconsequential to the reader. Assuming you work is something like altering diaries on the derivation of words got from old Aramaic, indeed, simply say that you have an altering position.

Correspondingly attempt to remember that anything can be placed down in two ways. You can either make it fascinating or exhausting; so work on it until you are certain that it won't exhaust a reader and the best test for this is hand it over to a dear companion and ask that companion's viewpoint. No one loves a drag so take all endeavors not to seem like one.


## TRUTH AND LIES

While you could take a consideration to cover your personality it is best not to lie.

Try not to attempt to feign your direction through a relationship in light of the fact that at some point the entire situation could emerge and obviously, one falsehood prompts another and afterward in no time the entire relationship will crash. Be as legit and as plain as possible, taking consideration to disguise your character.

Somebody once said that a companion is somebody who has a profound knowledge of you and loves you in any case. So there is compelling reason need to conceal things about you. Obviously you don't need to tell the individual each repulsive, violent insight concerning yourself, and yet you don't need to evoke stuff about you that simply isn't correct.

In the event that at all you in all actuality do lay out an exceptionally ruddy picture about yourself, including things that simply are false, or are unrealistic embellishments, and the other individual flips for you, truly you will luxuriate in someone else's greatness. This image you have painted is simply not you.

**EGO**

At the point when you pick a handle to distinguish yourself by, you must be sharp. Try not to attempt to draw in however many accomplices as would be prudent. All things considered, what are we searching for, quality or amount? Attempt to draw in just the sort of individuals you are keen on and who might think that you are fascinating.

To that end we recommended that you utilize a handle that better characterizes the sort of individual you are. Try not to attempt to seem like a sex god or a sex goddess. In the event that you are, let the other individual choose for him self or her self; (it is obviously superior to having the individual thought of proclamations like "is it in yet?") So avoid handles like Megastud, Handsomehunk, Superbabe or Bedlover.

Rather than that you could attempt handles that gives one a quick thought regarding the sort of individual you are. On the off chance that you are an outside individual use something like Natureguy or Naturegirl; in the event that you are a music freak use something like Musicman or Musicmaid. In the event that you are into theater and stuff like that you could pick a name like Theaterguy or Theatergirl.

The point is to prevail upon individuals who are keen on a similar stuff as you are. That obviously builds your possibilities of getting them.

## DO NOT WRITE EPISTLES

One more pivotal thing about composing your profile is that you ought to keep it as brief as could be expected. No one and that implies no one needs to peruse endlessly lines of someone else's profile. To whatever degree you cause it to be that way wordy the individual who is perusing it will get the possibility that you are the sort of individual who couldn't want anything more than to continue to discuss yourself and on second thought of go out on the town with you, the reader would prefer to twist up and kick the bucket.

Yet, that doesn't imply that you need to restrict the entire thing to only a couple of words. A too short profile would seem as though you lack the capacity to deal with this, yet you are simply doing it for its hell.

The best style that you could utilize is be 100 percent normal. Compose your profile as you would portray yourself to an individual straightforwardly. The discussion style has the largest allure I could add. Simplify it and avoid huge words and trite articulations.

## YOU ARE SPECIAL

Consider it briefly. Check out at yourself in the mirror. Do you appear as though any other individual that you know? We as a whole look so changed however basically we have been supplied with similar outside qualities, which are one nose, one mouth, two eyes and two ears.

So despite having similar structure blocks, in the event that we can look so changed for what reason do we need to sound the same? Ponder yourself another way. Try not to simply consider your preferences when you are composing your profile, think about your charming characteristics also. Charming characteristics, what are those?

Those will be those characteristics which make you loved by others. Obviously, these are things that we never trouble, about however perhaps we ought to. So what I would recommend is ask your closest companions for what valid reason they like you. Who knows, their responses could actually astound you! Be that as it may, basically you will find out about what you can remember for your profile.

You could evaluate the accompanying activity to figure out what sort of an individual you are. I won't say that the outcomes are totally secure however they surely may intrigue.

# STEP 3: BUILD THE RELATIONSHIP

Okay, so presently we are really prepared with our inclinations generally chalked out and our profiles posted. It is wonderful picture. It is practically similar to being situated alone at this elegant eatery, dressed to kill, with a glass of champagne in one hand and the other hand swung over the rear of the seat. You have a grin all the rage, a gleam in your expression and a greeting all over.

So what occurs straightaway? This individual who gives off an impression of being the ideal counterpart for you gets your attention and walks towards you. Presently what do you do? Kindly recollect that the portrayal above was relating to a virtual climate. Essentially, what we implied is that while you invest energy standing by in a chat room, this is the temperament that you will create.

So what happens when an individual takes the signal and starts chatting? Indeed, that truly is a shrewd inquiry. I might want to make one thing straight here. The Internet resembles some other roadway. It isn't protected until you get to feel comfortable around here. So what I would recommend is pay attention to your gut feelings and tread carefully. You can seem like an exceptionally warm individual however kindly be incredibly mindful about giving out any private data.

**SWEET PET NAMES**

Tell the other individual that you would like to be known by the handle you use or a better one, you could advise the individual to call you a pet name however let the individual in on that it is for sure a pet name, in light of the fact that sometime in the not too distant future, in the event that the relationship truly blooms it doesn't look decent assuming you need to express something like, "Well, unfortunately my name isn't actually Kate, it is Obadahun, I surmise I misled you."

The best thing for this situation is spread the word by the use of some famous names. You could call yourself Cinderella or Pocahontas or Archie, or Betty or Veronica. The chatting has now started and you can begin trading data. Keep to the general and avoid the particular.

## MEMORY

The human brain is to be sure something striking. It is fit for putting away and handling such an extensive variety of data that even a supercomputer would stay away when contrasted with it. Be that as it may, because of the virtual blast of data, our recollections have become exceptionally particular.

This implies that we can't recall all that we hear or see. Have little to no faith in your memory an excessive amount of with regards to chatting over the net. You could meet a many individuals over the net and you could chat with two or three them. So in the long run it could become challenging to recollect every one of them and their subtleties also.

Or on the other hand much more dreadful than that will be that you could end up being confounded and stir up subtleties. It would look terrible for you on the off chance that you call an individual some unacceptable name, or ask the individual some unacceptable subtleties. In such situations where you have been chatting with various people, for the wellbeing of paradise write down the insights concerning every individual independently or make separate records for every individual promotion store them in your PC.

At the point when you add them to your companions list use handles or nicknames that can assist you with recalling the individual the second you begin chatting sometime in the future.

Presently, on the off chance that you don't actually recollect the individual, then, at that point, it is unadvisable to play the speculating game. The other individual could get exceptionally outraged assuming you offer something like, "Is it Sarah or Mary?"

In such situations when you have a certified slip by of memory, the best thing to do is to be straightforward with the individual and say, "I realize we chatted a day or two ago, yet I'm horribly grieved, might you at any point kindly revive my memory about you?"

## SMALL TALK

There are few topics that are best for the initial talks so that an intimacy is not developed and at the same time you do not have to struggle for matters of common interest. You can talk about the weather, sports, movies, music and even food.

But at the same it is in bad taste to discuss religion, politics and family matters in the initial stages. You can crack jokes but dirty jokes are an absolute no-no at least in the first few talks.

Once you have talked more than once or twice and you feel comfortable with the person you can give the person your e-mail address but remember this is the first step towards virtual intimacy so you have to trust your instincts and nothing else. This takes things out of the public chat rooms and into the private inboxes.

**Instant Intimacy: watch out**

There are many individuals who feel that email won't ever have the glow or the individual bit of the antiquated letters and cards that individuals used to send through the postal assistance. That might be valid however email enjoys a benefit of the here and the at this point.

Since you know about the way that the individual you are chatting is contacting you similarly as you are connecting with that individual, there is an inclination for a closeness to develop even in a flash.

The medium fails to be the game changer and when an individual presses you for data which you need to supply promptly you could neglect specific subtleties out except if you are good to go.

You must be wary constantly and keep continually reminding your self that the individual you are chatting with is, after each of the a more peculiar and an integrity knows-what. Everything thing that you could manage is keep away from moment closeness by and large.

It doesn't exactly make any difference on the off chance that the other individual thinks that you are cold or held, you can undoubtedly tackle that by let the other individual know that it takes at some point for you to become OK with an individual. That truth be told is a decent quality since it is on par with saying,
"Indeed, I'm sorry I'm not the free kind who messes about."

There is something that a large number of my readers should be aware and that is the manner by which to see whether the other individual is lying. As I had let you know before, the Net can be an extremely perilous spot thus we must be certain beyond a shadow of a doubt about the honest intentions of the other individual prior to uncovering any private insights regarding ourselves. So the following part has been given explicitly for that.

# STEP 4: Finally Getting To Meet Each Other IN PERSON

Whenever you have begun talking once again the phone, then, at that point, the relationship has proactively taken wings, then, at that point, is no great explanation to defer an immediate gathering. So the thing would we say we are sitting tight for? However, stand by; there is compelling reason need to push it. You shouldn't sound over restless to meet this young lady or fellow.

Let the choice to meet develop over various calls. What's more, there are sure things that you can endure as a main priority before you truly meet.

## LOCATION

It isn't fitting to welcome somebody home before you have truly met the individual. You would be wise to pick a public spot ideally some place where there are a lot of individuals around, for good measure, you know.

For that reason most couples like to meet in an eatery over lunch or supper. There is one thing about having food together. At the point when individuals sit together and have food together they get to know a ton about one another.

Social graces enlighten us a ton regarding an individual's childhood and foundation and you can glean some significant experience about an individual by noticing the person in question eat. Subsequently, warm food magnificently affects the human brain. It delivers that multitude of stomach related squeezes and sets the tongue swaying. Individuals relax a great deal, particularly after a glass of wine or two.

The primary mix-up that the vast majority make is that they go under some unacceptable impression that a gathering, even the principal getting should end together in bed. No, it doesn't need to be so.

There is no impulse on your part or anybody's part that you need to bring the individual back home with you. Since you appreciate talking or visiting with an individual it doesn't be guaranteed to imply that you need to lay down with the individual. Allow that too to develop, so best to keep any such circumstances could prompt a bed room scene totally under control.

So how would you do that? The primary thing you ought to do is that you ought to be clear about the time. Nights are precarious times to meet. In the event that you eat together, there comes the chance of dropping the other individual home.

What's more, obviously you can't simply acknowledge a ride and leave subsequent to being dropped without welcoming the other individual in. And afterward one thing will prompt the other and afterward the unavoidable will undoubtedly occur. Obviously, on the off chance that that is the manner in which you would like it to be, you simply need to do everything I just said to you not to do.

Noon is the best time on the grounds that in the day time a large portion of us are occupied with work and we can simply save an hour or a half for lunch. So you can continuously leave on the appearance that you need to return to work or something to that effect. Not many individuals wind up returning home together after lunch. Something else is that at lunch the component of sentiment doesn't exactly come in.

Take care to be at the organized spot on time, you unquestionably don't have any desire to keep an individual you are meeting interestingly pausing. Dress properly for the event, keep it basic and yet it ought to be something that looks great on you.

## MAKE A DIFFERENCE

Presently, assume this date took care of business out as expected and you, as a matter of fact and completely partook in the organization of the other individual you could believe that the other individual should recollect you and ponder you, couldn't you? So how would you ensure that the other individual truly does contemplate you?

The response is basic. Simply make a meaningful difference . Bear in mind, a business or it isn't fitting here to visit card. It loans an extremely formal tone to the image. Certainly you don't maintain that the individual should recall you for your qualifications or your assignment. Something more customized would be more suitable.

Put your imaginative and inventive abilities into full stuff. In the event that you are idyllic, you could pen down a couple of lines on a little card and hand it to the individual. Granted, the lines ought not be about the individual, however about broad subjects like companionship, relationships, harmony, warmth, or gatherings. Be that as it may, do the writing ahead of time and save it for the right second. Try not to attempt to compose a sonnet on a paper napkin with the individual sitting before you!

In the event that you can't compose verse, perhaps you could get a few dried blossoms and stick them onto a card and duplicate down the lines of another person, yet concede that the lines are not your to the individual.

Save such a token with you and sit tight for the right second. Not long before you part, on the off chance that you are certain that "this is the one" hand it over to the individual with an extremely bashful demeanor all over and a shy, "I made this for you… " Believe me, it's miles better to say "I made this for you" than "I purchased this for you".

So what occurs if you are not excessively certain that you need to see this individual once more? Well save it with you itself and save it for the following individual.

On the off chance that the individual is the perfect individual, and assuming you gave the individual this customized token, the individual makes certain to think about you in a lot fonder manner.

## WARDROBE

You don't need to be dressed to kill when you venture out on a brief siesta. The best thing about get-togethers is that the majority of would be in our work garments and that saves us the distress of picking the correct thing to wear on a first date.

Something magnificent that you could do while going on a clench hand date is to make it a gathering movement, ideally a foursome. This removes the cumbersomeness of the circumstance and certainly removes that multitude of humiliating snapshots of quiet.

A gathering enjoys one more benefit in that lesser consideration will be centered around one another so there is less pressure and subsequently the two accomplices would be more loose. It is additionally more secure as well, since there is security in larger groups.

In any case, the organization to be incorporated ought to be commonly pleasing and not be pushed onto the other individual. In any case, take care to keep away from any individual who you know to be a motor-mouth; it removes all the tomfoolery in the event that one individual overwhelms the discussion.

You might drink assuming you need to, however don't drink a lot on your first date. In addition to the fact that it doesn't say well about when you are drunk, you could say something which you didn't intend to and that could destroy everything..

## THE BILL, WHO SETTLES IT

It's best to agree between yourself to pay for what you other. Even if things don't workout, no one will be obliged based on it.


## MULTIPLE DATES

So what occurs in the event that you get more than one proposal to date at pretty much a similar time? Or then again at the end of the day, what occurs in the event that you become near more than each individual in turn? Hello, that is presumably the very thing we are paying special attention to. You could go on various dates and afterward analyze for your self and pick the best individual.

You don't need to jump for the main individual who got your extravagant. You reserve the option to pick, so feel free to make it happen. There is compelling reason need to feel regretful around double crossing any body as long as you guarantee no one that you are not seeing any one else.

Furthermore, what occurs assuming that you find date No. 1 while you are out with date No.
2. Indeed, you should simply regard it as the most regular thing on the planet. Acquaint date No.1 with date No.2 as your companions and watch how they act. This is a brilliant approach to figuring out how an envious spouse might act in future.

Yet, what at any point occurs, a twofold date, that is going out with two individuals together is all the way impossible!

## DATING OFFLINE

At the point when you are dating online, you have a great deal of things for your potential benefit. For instance, the other individual doesn't actually see you and you don't actually need to make a fuss over appearances. You can commit your whole energy towards sounding keen and clever.

In any case, when you are really situated before an individual, there are 1,000 things that you need to focus on. There are many individuals who accept that keeping up appearances isn't exactly significant. They feel that acting naturally is more significant.

It sounds adequate. In any case, on your most memorable date basically you surely need to keep up appearances. The other individual shouldn't feel embarrassed to be seen around with you thus you ought to make a solid attempt as conceivable to stay away from that blooper.

Allow us to begin with your actual appearance. While I referenced before that you don't need to be dressed to kill, you genuinely must need to show up all around prepared. Take unique consideration about things like nails, hair, and teeth. Check for awful breath too in light of the fact that that to be sure is the most terrible mood killer.

What you wear ought not be clearly and draw in some unacceptable sort of consideration. Pick something that you are agreeable in and while looks great on you. Women, kindly be cautious about your make-up, and recollect that make-up is intended to emphasize your looks not to conceal it. Keeping away from ostentatious colors is ideal.

You ought to smell pleasant obviously yet don't over make it happen. We positively don't believe you should stay in the other individual's memory as only one in number smell. Men, if it's not too much trouble, take care to go in for manly aromas like musk, or scents from nature. Ladies, keep it as light and modest as could be expected.

**HOW TO USE YOUR CHARMS**

Everything that have been expressed so far are about how you can make a great impression. There is something that is similarly or significantly more significant than that, and that is to cause the other individual to feel great. Assist the other individual with unwinding.

A way you have been visiting for a long while so you really do know an extraordinary arrangement about one another. Everything thing you can manage is to facilitate the pressure and loosen things up. In some cases the ice gets so thick that you can in a real sense feel it. Split it up by telling a wisecrack or two.

Be that as it may, the joke ought to be unconstrained and with regards to the circumstance or, in all likelihood it will crash and burn. Try not to practice a joke in light of the fact that a practiced joke sounds… well… practiced.

The watchword here is fascinate. Utilize all the appeal that you can gather. Attempt to be as circumspect and as insightful as could really be expected. Try not to rule the discussion yet attempt to get the other individual talking. Individuals by and large love to discuss themselves so attempt to get the other individual talking by getting some information about the individual's work. Show interest in anything the other individual says.

Attempt to be a decent conversationalist. A decent conversationalist isn't an individual who talks well, however is one who listens well too. So attempt to be a decent audience. And keeping in mind that you are listening make an effort not to get occupied by something different or the other individual could feel that you are losing interest in what the person in question is talking about.

Then comes the inquiry, "what do you do assuming you observe that the other individual is overwhelming the discussion?"

All things considered, all things considered listen persistently briefly and afterward offer an inconspicuous hint like a cocked eyebrow or a grin through the side of your mouth. On the off chance that the other individual is adequately astute, the person in question will get the prompt. In the event that not, then take your risk, you could need to pay attention to this individual until the end of your life.

Humor seldom fizzles. Yet, again take care not to over make it happen. There is just something single more regrettable than an all out absence of humor and that is a lot of humor.


## PRESENTS AND GIFTS?

It is smart to take a gift alongside you as that makes a decent impression, however recall that when you are seeking the gifts ought to be restricted to flowers or chocolates only. While you are visiting attempt to figure out what the other individual preferences in flowers and chocolates. You absolutely don't have any desire to give the individual blossoms that the person is susceptible to.

The object of your gift ought not be to charm the individual yet to make a decent and enduring impression. There is no sense in going overboard a great deal on your most memorable date for there is no standard that everything ought to figure out well the initial time itself. Try not to over make it happen and simultaneously don't seem modest and miserly all things considered.

Anyway assuming the other individual has neglected to present to you a gift, rush to promise the individual that it is completely okay. Try not to allow the other individual to feel uncomfortable. As a matter of fact, that is a great method for making the discussion light. You can flippantly advise the other individual to get you a gift the following time.

# STEP 5: STAY STRONG

A large number of my readers may be stressed that everything doesn't figure out like has been depicted, how might they respond? Or on the other hand all in all on the off chance that this first date doesn't sort out how would it be advisable for them to respond?

The response is extremely basic, restart the entire cycle!

We should return to where we began. Keep in mind, this is an opportunity to track down the accomplice forever so we could need to develop many plants before we get the right gather.

I'm not discussing double crossing here. What I mean is that as opposed to tying up your resources in one place, keep the roads open. Try not to simply rely upon one individual, since, in such a case that that doesn't work out, you could lose heart. You can remain as optimistic as possible however anticipate the opposite too.

Just the each fortunate ones get the right pick at the main go it self. Until the end of us, we simply need to continue to attempt till we succeed. One more benefit of evaluating various individuals is that you can get to pick. It ought not be that you only flipped for the primary fellow or young lady who came your direction. Take you time, give yourself some breathing space and afterward pursue the ideal choice.

It's not possible for anyone to compel you into committing a responsibility. It ought to be totally your decision. Obviously, assuming you get the right prompts and something where it counts inside lets you know that this is the perfect individual for you, then, at that point, what are you sitting tight for, feel free to show the green sign.

In any case, then again in the event that somebody is attempting to compel you into earnestly committing to a responsibility and you feel frustrated, tenderly attempt to split away. Everything you need to do is put your foot down solidly and let the individual know that you want additional time.

Nonetheless, it isn't great to keep an individual standing by endlessly. Let the individual know that you want maybe seven days' time or more than that. Yet, don't allow the individual to understand that you are looking at others. Simply let them know that this is presumably the main choice in your life so you simply need no doubt.

## CONCLUSION

In the event that circumstances don't pan out kindly take care to smoothly part. In such occasions it isn't the most ideal choice to express such things over talk. The other individual might advance a few truly awkward inquiries that you will make some extreme memories replying.

The best thing you cold do is send the individual an email telling the person in question that the individual in question was not actually what you had as a main priority, yet you might want to stay old buddies no different either way.

You don't need to stress over being irritated by the other individual in future; the "old buddies" part won't ever fizzle. A great many people abhorrence to be known as an old buddy after a nearby experience. Generally speaking the relationship simply sizzles out after this. Anyway kindly recall that it is for sure terrible habits to leave behind out a word and quit noting sends with no data by any means.

Certain individuals would that since they really do like to annoy the other individual. However, such hardness is truly more regrettable.

So that is about it. You know all that will be known and the ball is currently well and genuinely in your courts. So the thing are you sitting tight for, how about you go out there and get back into the game with the catch that could only be described as epic.

I don't feel that we have left any stones unturned and from here I'm certain that on your most memorable date all that will be well in your control.

To your most memorable dating achievement online!

www.ingramcontent.com/pod-product-compliance
Lightning Source LLC
Chambersburg PA
CBHW060226170726
48004CB00004BA/1460